The Battle of Gettysburg

The Battle of Gettysburg

Dennis Brindell Fradin

Marshall Cavendish
Benchmark

New York

Dedication

For my granddaughter, Shalom Amelia Richard, with love

Marshall Cavendish Benchmark
99 White Plains Road
Tarrytown, NY 10591
www.marshallcavendish.us

Text and maps copyright © 2008 by Marshall Cavendish Corporation
Maps by XNR Productions

All Internet sites were available and accurate when sent to press.

Library of Congress Cataloging-in-Publication Data

Fradin, Dennis B.
The Battle of Gettysburg / Dennis Brindell Fradin.
p. cm. — (Turning points in U.S. history)
Includes bibliographical references and index.
ISBN-13: 978-0-7614-2043-9
1. Gettysburg, Battle of, Gettysburg, Pa., 1863—Juvenile literature. I. Title. II. Series.
E475.53.F7915 2007
973.7'349—dc22
2006025347

Photo research by Connie Gardner

Cover: A color lithograph depicting the Battle of Gettysburg, July 3, 1863
Title Page: A 1963 U.S. postage stamp commemorating the centennial of the Battle of Gettysburg

Cover Photo: MPI Stringer/Getty Images
Title Page: The Granger Collection

The photographs in this book are used by the permission and through the courtesy of: *North Wind Pictures:* 6, 19, 19, 36; *The Granger Collection:* 8, 16, 17, 18, 24, 26, 42; *Getty Images:* Hulton Archive, 23, 30; Corbis: 9, 12, 38; Bettmann, 10; Medford Historical Society Collection, 14; Matthew B. Brady Studio, 22.

Time Line: Dave Bartruff/CORBIS

Editor: Deborah Grahame
Publisher: Michelle Bisson
Art Director: Anahid Hamparian

Printed in Malaysia
1 3 5 6 4 2

Contents

This woodcut shows supporters of slavery burning antislavery documents in South Carolina during the 1830s.

CHAPTER ONE

A Nation Torn

The people of the United States clashed over slavery from the start. The **Declaration of Independence** announced the country's birth on July 4, 1776. Some Americans wanted the document to declare slavery evil or wrong, yet all thirteen states allowed slavery at the time. The nation's founders decided not to **denounce** slavery in the Declaration of Independence.

In 1787 American leaders met to create the new nation's constitution, or framework of government. Northern states had begun to end slavery by then.

An abolitionist is shown freeing a slave in this illustration from an antislavery almanac published in 1840.

Many Northern **delegates** insisted that the constitution ban slavery throughout the country. In the South, however, slavery was growing. Southern delegates threatened that they would not approve a constitution that outlawed slavery. To keep the peace the Northern delegates backed down. The **Constitution of the United States** did not outlaw slavery. It was approved by all thirteen original states.

The arguing over slavery continued, however. Between the early 1800s and 1860 it became even more heated. The **abolition movement** grew in the North. **Abolitionists** were determined to abolish, or end, slavery. The abolitionists spoke and wrote letters to protest against the practice. Some of them helped slaves escape from their owners. Meanwhile, Southern leaders spoke of states' rights. They believed each state should decide for itself whether or not to continue slavery.

People gathered at the Boston Common in 1851 to listen to an abolitionist speak against slavery.

Abraham Lincoln takes the oath of office during his inauguration as president in March 1861.

In November 1860 Abraham Lincoln was elected president of the United States. Southerners were afraid that he would try to end slavery.

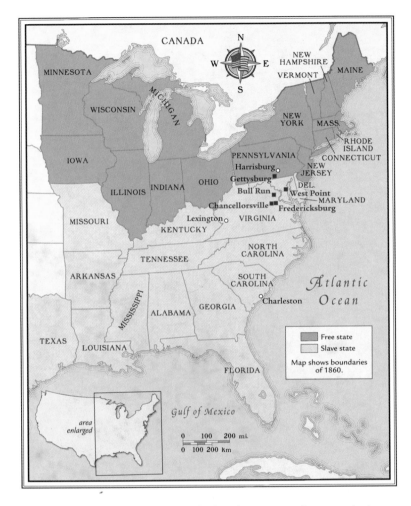

This map shows the boundaries between free and slave states in 1860.

Even before Lincoln took office as the sixteenth president, Southern states began to **secede,** or withdraw, from the United States. They formed their own country, the **Confederate States of America**. It was called the Confederacy or the South for short. The Confederates assembled an army, elected Jefferson Davis of Mississippi as president, and issued their own money.

The Confederacy must not be allowed to break away, President Lincoln believed. If states seceded whenever they disagreed with the government or disliked the results of an election, the United States would crumble. Besides, the Confederacy had seceded for a terrible reason—to continue slavery. The United States, also called the **Union** or the North, was determined to force the Confederacy back into the nation.

The attack on Fort Sumter in Charleston Harbor, South Carolina, marked the beginning of the Civil War. The fort is now a national monument.

What's That War Called?

Many Southerners called what is now known as the Civil War, the War of Northern Aggression. Many Northerners called it the War of Southern Rebellion.

Fighting began on April 12, 1861, when Confederates fired on a United States fort at Charleston, South Carolina. The Civil War was underway. Before ending four years later, it would claim more American lives than any other war in history.

Soldiers from the New York State Militia assembled in Harpers Ferry, Virginia, in an 1861 photograph.

CHAPTER TWO

"The War Will Be Over"

The Union had several advantages over the Confederacy. First, its population was much larger. At the war's start in 1861, the twenty-three Union states had more than 23 million people; the eleven Confederate states had only about 9 million people. Three and a half million Southerners were slaves, so this left only 5.5 million Southerners to support the Confederacy.

Its larger population helped the Union assemble a bigger army. During the war, 2.2 million men fought for the North. Less than half that many—900,000—served the Confederacy.

This poster urged recent immigrants to the United States to join the fight against Confederate forces.

Manufacturing was much more developed in the North than in the South. As a result, the Union government was better able to supply its army with clothing, weapons, and food. The Union's roads and railroads were also far superior. This made it easier for the Union to transport troops and supplies.

The Confederacy did have some things in its favor. Most white Southern boys learned to ride a horse and to hunt with a gun at a young age. Consequently, Southern men usually made fine soldiers. The South also had some outstanding generals, including Confederate army commander Robert E. Lee and Stonewall Jackson. On the other hand,

This drawing shows workers filling rifle cartridges for Union forces at the U.S. Arsenal in Watertown, Massachusetts.

Volunteer Confederate soldiers, also known as Rebels, gathered before the First Battle of Bull Run in 1861.

President Lincoln had trouble finding good generals early in the war. In addition, the South was physically large. The Union army had a hard time conquering such a major land mass.

During the war's first two years, several major battles ended in Confederate victories. The South won the First Battle of Bull Run, the Seven Days battles, the Second Battle of Bull Run, and the Battle of Fredericksburg, all fought in Virginia in 1861 and 1862.

In May 1863 Confederates under Robert E. Lee won another stunning victory at Chancellorsville, Virginia. However, Stonewall Jackson died as a result of wounds suffered in this battle. Lee commented

Robert E. Lee

Robert Edward Lee was born in Virginia's Westmoreland County. He graduated from West Point, the United States Military Academy in New York State.

In early 1861 President Lincoln asked Lee to command the Northern army. Lee disliked slavery. He had freed his own slaves and opposed Southern secession. Still, he would not fight his fellow Southerners. He turned Lincoln down and instead became the Confederate commander. Even though Lee made some questionable decisions at Gettysburg, his military genius helped the South put up a terrific fight against a much larger force in the Civil War.

Lee later served as president of Washington College in Lexington, Virginia.

Robert Edward Lee (1807–1870)

This drawing from a Northern newspaper shows Confederate troops attacking Northern soldiers during the First Battle of Bull Run.

Stonewall Jackson

Thomas Jonathan Jackson earned his famous nickname during the Civil War. He and his men became known for holding their ground like a stone wall. Some people claim the Confederates could have won the Battle of Gettysburg if General Stonewall Jackson had been there to help Lee. But two months earlier Jackson had been accidentally shot by his own men, who mistook him for the enemy. Jackson had died eight days later.

about Jackson's death, "I do not know how to replace him."

After the Battle of Chancellorsville, General Lee decided to invade the North and marched his Confederate army into Pennsylvania. Beating the Union troops on their home soil might convince the Northerners to give up the fight. Also, Southern troops could obtain food and supplies from Northern farms and towns.

Lee's Confederate troops entered Pennsylvania in June 1863. The Union army followed the Confederates northward. The two armies met at Gettysburg, a crossroads town of 2,400 people.

George Gordon Meade

Born in Spain of American parents, George Gordon Meade graduated from West Point and served in the Mexican War. After the Civil War began, Meade led Pennsylvania volunteers. He fought in a number of major battles. On June 28, 1863, President Lincoln named him commander of the Union army.

Considering that he had just three days to prepare, Meade did an outstanding job at the Battle of Gettysburg. His **strategy** of holding the high ground resulted in a Union victory. Because of Meade's outbursts when he was upset, his men called him Old Snapping Turtle.

George Gordon Meade (1815–1872)

General Stonewall Jackson, left, and General Robert E. Lee, right, are shown during their last meeting before Jackson's death at the Battle of Chancellorsville in 1863.

General George G. Meade, who now commanded the Union army, led 90,000 troops. Lee's forces stood at 75,000. The Confederates had won so often that General Lee was confident of victory. Lee told one of his officers that he expected to "crush" the Union forces at Gettysburg and then "virtually destroy," the Northern army. "The war will be over and we shall achieve the recognition of our independence!" General Lee boldly predicted.

The ferocious fighting and huge loss of life at the Battle of Gettysburg has inspired generations of writers and artists. The battle is depicted in this lithograph by Currier and Ives.

CHAPTER THREE

The Stream Ran Red

The fighting at Gettysburg broke out early on Wednesday, July 1, 1863. Reportedly, a Union cavalryman, or horse soldier, from Illinois fired the opening shot at a group of Confederates. This began the most tremendous battle ever fought in North or South America.

The deadly struggle lasted three days. The two sides fought in the open, from behind trees, and in headlong **charges**. They fired rifles and cannons at each other. Occasionally they fought hand-to-hand with bayonets—knife-like weapons attached to gun barrels.

Brigadier General George Armstrong Custer (1839–1876) saw action in the Civil War, including the Battles of Chancellorsville, Bull Run, and Gettysburg.

The battle was really many separate fights. There was **military** action at McPherson's Ridge, hills called Little Round Top and Big Round Top, the Peach Orchard, a rocky area called Devil's Den, and Culp's Hill. Part of the fighting on July 1 took place in the streets of Gettysburg.

Some famous military figures led the opposing forces. Besides Robert E. Lee, the Confederate generals at Gettysburg included James Longstreet, Richard Ewell, and Jeb Stuart. Besides George G. Meade, the Union generals included George Armstrong Custer, Abner Doubleday, and Winfield Scott Hancock.

There were many reminders that the enemies—North and South— had once been friends. For example, Paul Revere of Massachusetts and Henry Lee of Virginia had both been Revolutionary War heroes. Revere had warned Americans that the British were coming before the

Revolution's first battle. Henry "Light-Horse Harry" Lee had led cavalry raids against the British. Now, nearly ninety years later, Light-Horse Harry's son, Robert E. Lee, was the Confederate commander. Paul Revere's grandson, Paul Joseph Revere, was a Union officer from Massachusetts. Colonel Revere was wounded on July 2. He died three days later.

The fighting at Gettysburg was fierce during the first two days of the battle. The following descriptions were written by soldiers on opposing sides:

"O, THE DIN AND THE ROAR"

*A bullet hissed by my cheek so close that I felt the movement of the air. Now began the countless flashes, and the long fiery sheets of the muskets, mingled with the thunder of the guns. O, the din and the roar, what a hell is there! Men are dropping dead or wounded on all sides, by scores and by hundreds, and the poor **mutilated** creatures, some with an arm dangling, some with a leg broken by a bullet, are limping and crawling toward the rear.*

Frank A. Haskell, a Union soldier from Wisconsin

"BULLETS THICK AS HAILSTONES"

*The **Yankees** were advancing, and death had
commenced his work. The battle now rages furiously,
but our lines move straight onward. The roaring of
artillery, bullets thick as hailstones, men falling on
every side, yet we succeed in breaking their first and
second lines of battle. At the third and last line, we
met stern resistance, [Union troops who] fought with bravery.
Under the terrible fire they did not run, returning our fire,
but leaving the ground covered with their dead.*

Edmund DeWitt Patterson, a Confederate soldier from Alabama

After two days of fighting, General Lee's prediction about crushing
the enemy had not come true. Instead, the Northerners had surprised the
Confederates by bravely defending their home soil. So far the battle was a
stalemate. Each side had experienced some gains and setbacks while
suffering huge losses. A total of nearly 33,000 men had been killed or

Union soldiers successfully defended their position on the hill later called "Little Round Top."

wounded on July 1 and 2. A stream in the area called Plum Run turned red because hundreds of men cleaned their bloody wounds in the water.

Yet neither side was ready to quit. Another day of fighting would decide the Battle of Gettysburg.

Pickett's Charge was a turning point in the Battle of Gettysburg and gave the victory to Union forces.

CHAPTER FOUR

Pickett's Charge

As July 3 dawned, General Meade's Union army held the high ground of Cemetery Ridge. However, General Lee believed that victory was still within reach. Lee made a daring plan. Confederate forces would charge across a mile-long field toward the Union soldiers. They would overwhelm the Northerners and send them fleeing as in earlier battles—so Lee hoped.

Confederate general James Longstreet told Lee the plan would not work. The Northerners' position on high ground was too strong. However, Lee was convinced that his forces would triumph. "The enemy is there and I am going to strike him!" General Lee declared.

General George Pickett was to lead the Confederate charge. Before Pickett's attack, Lee wanted to weaken the Union forces. At 1:00 P.M. on July 3, 1863, about 150 Confederate cannons began firing at the Northerners. Witnesses said the two-hour **bombardment** produced the loudest man-made noise that had ever been heard in North America. People forty miles away in Harrisburg, Pennsylvania, heard the noise. "It seemed as though all the artillery in the universe had opened fire and was belching forth its missiles of death and destruction," reported a Union soldier from Connecticut.

At about 3:00 P.M. the bombardment ended. "Men, to your posts!" General Pickett told his troops. Fourteen thousand Confederates began to advance toward the Northerners. Some rode on horseback, but most of the Confederates made Pickett's Charge on foot.

The Union soldiers could hardly believe their eyes. "An ocean of armed men swept upon us!" recalled Lieutenant Frank A. Haskell. The nearly mile-wide army of attackers "moved toward us like an avalanche," reported another Northerner.

The Confederates kept advancing, but the Union men held their position. When the Confederates were 1,200 yards away, the Union forces pounded them with cannon fire. Many of the Southerners were killed or wounded, yet still the charge continued. When the Confederates were one hundred yards away, the Northerners began attacking them with rifle fire.

George Pickett

Born in Richmond, Virginia, George Pickett (1825–1875) graduated last in his class of fifty-nine at West Point. Nonetheless, he became a fine soldier. Pickett was a hero of the Mexican War. Later, he was stationed in the Northwest, where he learned the Native Americans' languages and became their teacher.

When the Civil War began, Pickett joined the Confederate army and rose to the rank of general. In mid-1862 he was severely wounded and was out of action for six months. A handsome man who wore his hair in shoulder-length curls, Pickett led the most famous attack of the Civil War: Pickett's Charge at the Battle of Gettysburg. Afterward, he tried to comfort his troops but could only cry, "My brave men! My brave men!"

It was said that Pickett never forgave Robert E. Lee for sending so many of his men to their death. Once the war ended, Pickett worked as an insurance salesman in Richmond, Virginia.

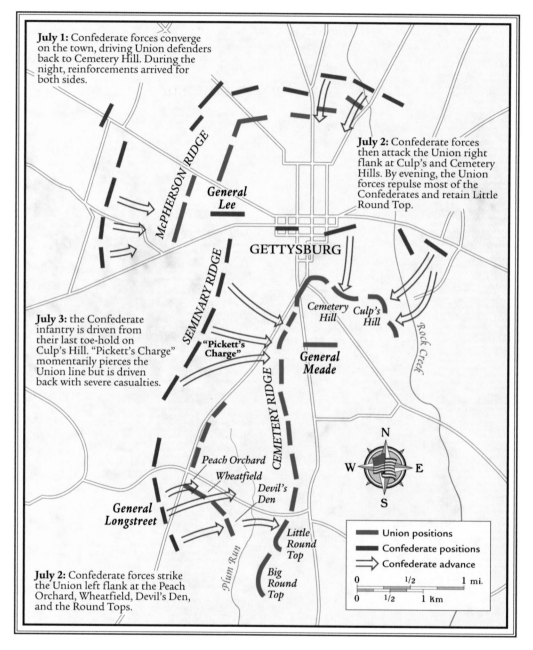

July 1: Confederate forces converge on the town, driving Union defenders back to Cemetery Hill. During the night, reinforcements arrived for both sides.

July 2: Confederate forces then attack the Union right flank at Culp's and Cemetery Hills. By evening, the Union forces repulse most of the Confederates and retain Little Round Top.

McPHERSON RIDGE

General Lee

SEMINARY RIDGE

GETTYSBURG

July 3: the Confederate infantry is driven from their last toe-hold on Culp's Hill. "Pickett's Charge" momentarily pierces the Union line but is driven back with severe casualties.

"Pickett's Charge"

Cemetery Hill *Culp's Hill*

Rock Creek

General Meade

CEMETERY RIDGE

Peach Orchard

Wheatfield

Devil's Den

N
W   E
S

General Longstreet

Plum Run

Little Round Top

Big Round Top

July 2: Confederate forces strike the Union left flank at the Peach Orchard, Wheatfield, Devil's Den, and the Round Tops.

	Union positions
	Confederate positions
	Confederate advance

0   1/2   1 mi.

0   1/2   1 Km

This map charts the movements of Confederate and Union forces during the three-day battle.

By the hundreds, then the thousands, Pickett's men were shot down. More than half of the Confederate attackers were killed, wounded, or captured in the famous charge. Finally, the survivors had to turn around and retreat through the field they had just crossed.

"Oh the dead and the dying on this bloody field," wrote a soldier who witnessed the July 3 fighting.

The defeat of Pickett's Charge meant that the Union had won the Battle of Gettysburg. When General Meade rode out to the field and saw the results, he said, "Thank God!"

A mile away General Lee rode out to meet the survivors of the charge. "It is all my fault!" he said to them. He told one of his officers that he had never seen anything braver than Pickett's Charge.

The next day General Lee began to withdraw what was left of his army from Pennsylvania.

General Lee leads his men home as they retreat from the bloody battlefield.

CHAPTER FIVE

Aftermath

The day after the Battle of Gettysburg was the eighty-seventh birthday of the United States. There were celebrations in the North for the victory at Gettysburg, but in many ways it was a grim Fourth of July. Never had such a brutal battle been fought in the Americas. In the three-day clash the South had suffered 28,000 and the North 23,000 casualties—men killed, wounded, captured, and missing. The death toll stood at about 3,900 for the South and 3,150 for the North. The toll climbed over the next weeks as many wounded men died.

Visitors to the battlefield were sickened by what they saw. The cannon and rifle fire had been so destructive that many bodies scarcely looked human. Strewn about the battlefield were human arms, legs, and heads. About two thousand horses were also dead.

The Union victory at Gettysburg was a turning point in the Civil War. The Confederacy could not replace the officers, soldiers, and supplies lost at Gettysburg. Never again would the Confederates make a major invasion of the North. In fact, never again would the South have the strength to conduct a major campaign of attack against Union forces.

Dead soldiers, due to be buried at Rose Farm near Gettysburg, photographed July 5, 1863.

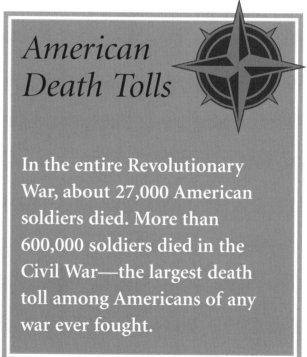

American Death Tolls

In the entire Revolutionary War, about 27,000 American soldiers died. More than 600,000 soldiers died in the Civil War—the largest death toll among Americans of any war ever fought.

The Gettysburg Address

On November 19, 1863, a cemetery for fallen Union soldiers was dedicated at the Gettysburg battlefield. President Lincoln made a brief speech at the ceremony. "Four **score** and seven years ago our fathers brought forth on this continent, a new nation, conceived in liberty, and dedicated to the proposition that all men are created equal," he began. The Union was fighting the war so that the "nation might live," Lincoln went on to say. He concluded by proclaiming, "We here highly resolve that these dead shall not have died in vain—that this nation, under God, shall have a new birth of freedom—and that government of the people, by the people, for the people, shall not perish from the earth." Lincoln's short talk is called the Gettysburg Address. It became the most famous speech in U.S. history.

Although the victory at Gettysburg helped the Union win the war, the fighting continued for nearly two full years. During that time the war claimed more lives than those lost up to and including the Battle of Gettysburg. Not until 1865 did the Civil War end. That year the remaining slaves were freed and the two sides began the process of reuniting as one nation.

Glossary

abolition movement—The movement to end slavery.

abolitionists—People who want to end slavery.

artillery—Cannons and other large firing weapons.

bombardment—An attack using bombs or shells.

charges—Military attacks in which troops advance quickly toward the enemy.

Confederate States of America (Confederacy)—The country composed of the eleven Southern states that seceded from the Union.

Constitution of the United States—The framework of government for the United States. It was created in 1787 and took effect in 1788.

Declaration of Independence—The document, issued in 1776, announcing that the thirteen colonies had become the United States of America.

delegates—People who act for other people.

denounce—To announce threateningly; to declare evil.

manufacturing—The making of products.

military—Relating to soldiers or war.

mutilated—Cut up; destroyed.

score—An old word for the number twenty; when Abraham Lincoln said "four score and seven" in the Gettysburg Address, he meant eighty-seven.

secede—To leave or withdraw from a country or organization.

stalemate—A deadlock or tie.

strategy—A careful plan.

Union—A commonly used name for the United States or for the North during the Civil War period.

Yankee—A nickname for Northerners.

Timeline

1607—Virginia, England's first permanent American colony, is founded

1733—Georgia, England's thirteenth American colony, is founded

1776—**July 4:** The Declaration of Independence, announcing that the thirteen colonies have become the United States of America, is approved

1780—Massachusetts becomes the first of the original thirteen states to end slavery

1787—American leaders create the new nation's framework of government, the Constitution of the United States

1788—**June 21:** The U.S. Constitution goes into effect
Late 1700s–mid 1800s—Northerners and Southerners argue over slavery

1850—Out of total U.S. population of 23 million, there are 3.2 million slaves, mostly in the South

1860—**November 6:** Abraham Lincol is elected president
December 20: South Carolina become the first state to secede; eventually eleven states secede and become the Confederate States of America

1607   *1776*   *1860*

1861—April 12: The Civil War begins with the Confederate attack on Fort Sumter in South Carolina

1863—July 1–3: The Battle of Gettysburg ends in Union victory **November 19**: President Lincoln delivers the Gettysburg Address

1865—April 9: The Union wins the Civil War; more than 600,000 soldiers have died, the most American deaths of any war ever fought **April 15:** President Lincoln, shot by John Wilkes Booth, dies **December 6:** The Thirteenth Amendment to the U.S Constitution ends slavery

1870—All former Confederate states have been readmitted to the Union

1933—The National Park Service takes over management of Gettysburg National Military Park

1963—One-hundredth anniversary of the Battle of Gettysburg

1970—One-hundredth anniversary of the rejoining of all the states in the Union

2013—150th anniversary of the Battle of Gettysburg

1863   *1870*

Further Information

B O O K S

Ashby, Ruth. *Gettysburg*. North Mankato, MN: Smart Apple Media, 2002.

Crewe, Sabrina, and Dale Anderson. *The Battle of Gettysburg*. Milwaukee, WI: Gareth Stevens, 2003.

DeAngelis, Gina. *The Battle of Gettysburg: Turning Point of the Civil War*. Mankato, MN: Capstone Press, 2003.

Ford, Carin T. *The Battle of Gettysburg and Lincoln's Gettysburg Address*. Berkeley Heights, NJ: Enslow, 2004.

W E B   S I T E S

First of a three-page site describing the Battle of Gettysburg, sponsored by the Gettysburg Welcome Center
www.gettysbg.com/battle.shtml

The National Park Service's Gettysburg National Military Park site
www.nps.gov/gett

A summary of the Battle of Gettysburg, including an eyewitness description by teenager Tillie (Pierce) Alleman
www.eyewitnesstohistory.com/pfgtburg.htm

This description of the Battle of Gettysburg includes a link to post-battle photos
www.historyplace.com/lincoln/battle.htm

Bibliography

Boritt, Gabor S., ed. *The Gettysburg Nobody Knows.* New York: Oxford University Press, 1997.

Catton, Bruce. *Gettysburg: The Final Fury.* Garden City, NY: Doubleday, 1974.

Gramm, Kent. *Gettysburg: A Meditation on War and Values.* Bloomington: Indiana University Press, 1994.

Haskell, Frank Aretas. *The Battle of Gettysburg,* second ed. Madison: Wisconsin History Commission, 1910.

Symonds, Craig L. *American Heritage History of the Battle of Gettysburg.* New York: HarperCollins, 2001.

Tackach, James, ed. *The Battle of Gettysburg.* San Diego: Greenhaven Press, 2002.

Index

Page numbers in **boldface** are illustrations.

About the Author

Dennis Fradin is the author of 150 books, some of them written with his wife, Judith Bloom Fradin. Their recent book for Clarion, *The Power of One: Daisy Bates and the Little Rock Nine*, was named a Golden Kite Honor Book. Another of Dennis's recent books is *Let It Begin Here! Lexington & Concord: First Battles of the American Revolution*, published by Walker. The Fradins are currently writing a biography of social worker and antiwar activist Jane Addams for Clarion, and a nonfiction book about a slave escape for National Geographic Children's Books. Turning Points in U.S. History is Dennis Fradin's first series for Marshall Cavendish Benchmark. The Fradins have three grown children and three young grandchildren.